Original title:
Moments To Hold Close

Copyright © 2024 Swan Charm Publishing
All rights reserved.

Editor: Jessica Elisabeth Luik
Author: Mirell Mesipuu
ISBN HARDBACK: 978-9916-86-122-6
ISBN PAPERBACK: 978-9916-86-123-3

Delicate Echoes

In the hush of twilight
whispers soft and bright,
timeless echoes call
thrilled with silent light.

Across the ancient trees
secrets in the breeze,
small voices linger there
within the shadows glistening free.

Captured Heartbeats

In the space where hearts entwine,
and dreams are spun with gold,
our pulses gently rhyme
a dance of love retold.

Each beat a tender pledge
a promise softly sworn,
moments evergreen,
two souls forever borne.

Elusive Kisses

In the world of fleeting dreams
kisses hide unseen,
between the dawn and dusk,
a love so bright and keen.

Elusive as the mist
they fade with morning light,
whispers on the lips
disappearing into the night.

Sweet Nostalgia

Beneath the pale moon's glow
memory's gentle stream,
nights of yesteryears
whisper in a dream.

Caress of time gone by
moments wrapped in gold,
sweet nostalgia sighs,
stories warm and old.

Cerulean Hues

Beneath the sky, in cerulean hues,
Oceans whisper their ancient news.
Waves dance with a rhythmic grace,
In endless blue, they find their place.

Birds soar high, in azure flights,
Painting the heavens with delicate sights.
Clouds drift by, in shapes so grand,
A canvas of dreams, where hopes expand.

Mountains rise, with peaks so bold,
Guardians of secrets, both new and old.
Rivers flow, with crystal streams,
In cerulean hues, we find our dreams.

Fading Glimmers

In the quiet dusk, where shadows meet,
Fading glimmers weave a silent feat.
Stars emerge, like whispered beams,
Lighting up our twilight dreams.

Moon ascends, with a gentle wane,
Casting silver on the earthly plain.
Fireflies flicker, in meadows wide,
In this soft glow, our fears subside.

Night embraces, with velvet touch,
Holding secrets, cherished so much.
Morn will come, with golden rays,
But for now, in glimmers, our heart stays.

Timeless Flickers

Candles burn, with delicate flames,
Flickers dance, like tender frames.
In their glow, time seems to cease,
Moments captured, in perfect peace.

Eyes reflect, the warm embrace,
In their light, we find our place.
Whispers soft, in shadows play,
Timeless beauty, night and day.

Hearts align, in gentle hours,
Where love blooms, like fragile flowers.
In these flickers, dreams ignite,
Guiding souls through endless night.

Sunset Reveries

Golden rays, as sun descends,
Mark the time when day suspends.
Horizons painted, hues so bright,
Whispered dreams take flight.

Silhouettes, in amber glow,
Cast their shadows, soft and slow.
The world prepares for twilight's kiss,
A moment wrapped in bliss.

Colors blend, in muted tones,
Nature's canvas, where beauty's sown.
In sunset's warm, embracing gleam,
We lose ourselves in reverie and dream.

Moments Etched in Time

In silver shards of evening light,
Memories whisper through the night,
Traces of laughter, shadows cast,
Imprints of a fond, distant past.

Footprints along the sandy shore,
Songs and stories, old folklore,
Winds carry tales, both near and far,
Moments shine like evening stars.

In hearts, they linger, softly glow,
Time erodes them, yet they show,
In dreams, they bloom, a temporal garden,
Moments etched, no need for pardon.

Silent echoes through the years,
Bind our joys and long-lost fears,
Threads of time, a woven quilt,
Of love and paths, destiny built.

When darkness wraps the valiant blue,
Those etched moments remain true,
In every dawn and twilight's gleam,
They're scripted into life's grand dream.

Inner Sanctuaries

In the quiet of a serene glade,
Where shadows dance, sunlight played,
Hearts find solace, minds retreat,
In sanctuaries, time depletes.

Whispers of winds, the gentle touch,
Nature's hymn, saying much,
Pools of peace, reflections bright,
Inner sanctuaries, pure delight.

In silent woods where pathways weave,
Thoughts unwind, spirits believe,
Harmony of the world's fine thread,
Softly cradles nights ahead.

The soul resides in tranquil lore,
In corners unseen, keeping score,
In spaces where the calm proceeds,
Inner sanctuaries, hushed needs.

By flickering flames of inner fires,
Smolders dreams and old desires,
In sanctums guarded from the strife,
There we rediscover life.

Golden Threads

Threads of gold in the tapestry,
Woven tales of you and me,
In every stitch, in every line,
Promises of love entwine.

Golden threads of memories past,
Through time's loom, they hold fast,
Binding hearts in silken ties,
Underneath the azure skies.

In sunlit mornings, wake the hues,
Of dreams, ambitions, scattered clues,
These golden threads our lives bestow,
Moments grand and whispers low.

Through joy and tears, the fabric gleams,
Embroidered with our hopes and dreams,
Each thread a story, rich and bold,
In life's design, these strands unfold.

In future's gaze, the tales extend,
With golden threads that never end,
Our lives a woven artistry,
Bound by love, eternally.

Moments in Mosaic

Fragments of life's grand design,
Moments like a mosaic shrine,
Each piece a memory held dear,
Together forming visions clear.

In the dance of dusk and dawn,
Mosaics of a life long gone,
Colors blend through time's embrace,
Crafted with a gentle grace.

Anguish and joy, their colors bright,
Mingle in the softest light,
Patterned on the soul's vast canvas,
Moments in a grand, vibrant dance.

Each shard a tale, a whispered song,
In the mosaic where we belong,
Fragments that do gently connect,
Create a life of deep respect.

Glistening through the endless years,
A mosaic of laughter, love, and tears,
In every glance, in each small token,
Moments in mosaic, silently spoken.

Awakened With Light

Morning's first kiss, a tender embrace,
Golden hues splash, shadows they chase.
Birds on the wing, songs they bestow,
Whispering secrets only dawn can know.

Nature awakens, petals unfurl,
In the hush of dawn, dreams start to swirl.
Crimson and amber paint the sky bright,
A world reborn, awakened with light.

Mountains stand tall, shrouded in mist,
The sun ascends, by clouds gently kissed.
Rivers of gold through the valleys meander,
A symphony of light, a soft, sweet pander.

Leaves on the trees, whispering tales,
Of fluttering wings and soft morning gales.
With every sunrise, hope embarks its flight,
Chasing the shadows, embracing the light.

In the embrace of the morning serene,
Every moment feels like a timeless scene.
Hearts are renewed with every sun's rise,
In dawn's embrace, beneath radiant skies.

Breeze Kissed Days

Whispers of wind, through branches they glide,
Carrying tales from places far and wide.
The scent of blossoms, carried so free,
On breeze kissed days, tranquility's decree.

Softly they dance, the leaves in the air,
Each gentle gust a moment to share.
With each breath taken, fond memories trace,
In the tender caress of nature's embrace.

Clouds drifting by, like ships in the sky,
Over fields and meadows, they quietly fly.
Shadows cast gently, cool touches of grace,
In the warm, tender glow of sun's embrace.

Rivers of air, they weave and they spin,
Tickling the grass, playing with kin.
Each rustle a promise, a soft serenade,
On breeze kissed days, where dreams are made.

Under the canopy, swayed by the breeze,
Time stands still, moments freeze.
With hearts alight and spirits raised,
We find peace in these breeze kissed days.

Ephemeral Love

In fleeting whispers, love finds its way,
A transient dance, by night and by day.
Moments of passion, swiftly they fly,
Ephemeral love, like clouds in the sky.

Tender embraces, brief and so sweet,
Two souls entwined, where worlds softly meet.
Fragile as petals, yet deep as the sea,
In those fleeting moments, we are set free.

Echoes of laughter, fading in the dawn,
A melody played, hearts tightly drawn.
Just like the sunset, with colors ablaze,
Ephemeral love, in fleeting displays.

Glimpses of forever, in each fleeting glance,
A waltz of the hearts, in a transient dance.
Though moments may fade, memories they keep,
In the realms of the mind, they forever seep.

Time gently whispers, as love softly sighs,
In the ephemeral dance, beneath twilight skies.
For love's brief moments, our hearts will yearn,
Like the briefest flame, forever it will burn.

Twilight Reverie

The sky paints hues of lavender and gold,
As day surrenders to the silent night.
Stars emerge like stories to be told,
In twilight's gentle, calming light.

Soft whispers of the breeze gently twirl,
Dancing through the leaves with silent grace.
Each moment holds a dream, a precious pearl,
In twilight's tender, warm embrace.

The colors fade, the night grows deep,
A world in shadows softly sways.
In twilight's arms, we fall asleep,
Dreamers of the hidden rays.

Embraced Realities

Leaves listen to the voices of the wind,
Narratives of life's untamed cascade.
Messengers of truths softly pinned,
In the essence where dreams invade.

Hopes and fears blend in twilight's glow,
Courage whispers in the darkest night.
Embrace the ebb and flow,
Of reality's resilient light.

Time chisels moments into stone,
Sculpting lives with a master's hand.
In the silence, the heart is known,
And dreams are built on shifting sand.

Colloquial Winks

Beneath the banter and the cheerful jest,
Lies wisdom nestled in the ordinary.
Life's simple tales, often expressed,
In the language of the voluntary.

Eyes speak where words may falter,
Winks narrate unspoken lore.
Understanding in the unlettered altar,
Of shared histories and more.

In colloquial winks, secrets rest,
Mirth and meaning intertwined.
Hearts in amusement are blessed,
In the common joys we find.

Whispered Echoes

In the quiet, echoes softly speak,
Of passive dreams and thoughts untold.
Murmurs of hearts both strong and weak,
In whispers of the gentle and bold.

Shadows cast by yesterday's light,
Dance in whispers of memory's lane.
Silent songs of love, of fight,
Echoes of joy and whispered pain.

Within the silence, stories bloom,
Of laughter and the tears we sow.
In whispered echoes, beyond the gloom,
Life's eternal pulse continues to flow.

Whispers of the Past

Beneath the ancient sycamore's shade,
Echoes of yesteryears softly played.
Memories drift like leaves in the breeze,
Carrying tales of forgotten seas.

Voices murmur in the twilight's gleam,
Fragments of an old, long-lost dream.
Time-worn faces in shadows cast,
Revealing secrets from the past.

Silent whispers float on the air,
Whispering stories beyond compare.
Their soft cadence, a gentle embrace,
Binding us to a distant place.

In the hush of the evening's glow,
These whispers of the past bestow.
Traces of love, of joy, and pain,
Etched in the heart, time and again.

Holding Ephemera

Moments fleeting like morning mist,
Grip them tightly, they still resist.
Pictures yellowed, letters worn,
Memories of a love once sworn.

Each token a sacred affair,
Hints of magic in the thin air.
Feathers light from a nameless bird,
Each with a silent, whispering word.

Footprints vanish in shifting sands,
Ephemera slipping through hands.
But their weight, though light they seem,
Anchor us in a timeless dream.

Echoes held in fragile repose,
A blossom's scent, a distant rose.
These fleeting treasures in our hold,
Stories ephemeral, yet bold.

Whisked Away

Clouds curl and twist in silent flight,
Drawing the eye to the boundless height.
Dreams whisper on the wind's soft sigh,
Whisking the heart to a distant sky.

Waves crash on an unseen shore,
Inviting us to see much more.
The ocean's depth, a siren's call,
Beckoning us to rise and fall.

Stars ignite the evening's soft veil,
Guiding souls on an astral trail.
Each twinkle tells a lore untold,
Of journeys vast and hearts so bold.

We leap into this sacred space,
Leaving behind the human race.
Whisked away on wings of air,
To realms unknown, beyond compare.

Golden Fragments

Sunlight dances on the waves below,
Breaking into fragments that softly glow.
Each piece a shard of golden light,
Scattering warmth into the night.

Glimmers on the surface wide,
Whispers of a celestial tide.
Fragments of dreams set adrift,
In cosmic currents, they slowly lift.

Leaves catch fire in the autumn's breath,
Golden hues heralding life's death.
Yet in each fragment life begins anew,
A cycle eternal, ever true.

Hearts hold these golden shards so dear,
Fragments of love that persevere.
Each piece a memory, fond and bright,
Illuminating the endless night.

Heartbeats Preserved

In shadows of time, our heartbeats remain,
Echoes of laughter, whispers in pain.
Memories painted with colors so bright,
In the gallery of soul, preserved in the light.

Each pulse a rhythm, a silent refrain,
Moments captured in droplets of rain.
Binding us through stories untold,
In fragments of warmth, our hands still hold.

Unseen but felt, like a gentle breeze,
Woven in chapters, written with ease.
Promises linger, through ages conserved,
In the essence of life, heartbeats preserved.

Magic in A Breath

Inhale the morning, fresh and pristine,
Whispers of sunlight in a golden sheen.
With every breath, a new spell is cast,
Moments enchanted, slow and vast.

The world breathes magic, subtle, unseen,
Through the rustling leaves, in the air serene.
Life unfurls in delicate wreath,
There's magic dwelling, in each breath we breathe.

Depths of the ocean, the breeze's caress,
Magic alights in the heart's recess.
In the soft exhale, dreams coalesce,
Life is but moments, in breaths we confess.

Fleeting Yet Forever

Stars blaze brightly in the evening sky,
Ephemeral glimmers that catch the eye.
Moments so fleeting, yet there they stay,
Carved in our hearts, forever and a day.

Petals may fall as seasons turn,
Yet love in our hearts will forever burn.
In whispers of wind, memories tether,
Life is a dance, fleeting yet forever.

In the swift passage of night to dawn,
Beauty is found, in each fleeting song.
While moments fade, intertwined together,
Love remains, fleeting, yet forever.

Embraced Highlights

In the tapestry of moments we share,
Bright highlights of love beyond compare.
Embraced by joy in the light of day,
In the shadows of dusk, they softly stay.

Sparkling eyes in a midnight's gleam,
Embraced by stars, a lover's dream.
Every highlight, a memory's delight,
In the embrace of love, take flight.

Through peaks and valleys, side by side,
Embraced by the journey, our hearts confide.
Among the highlights, in purest light,
Our lives converge, in love's grand sight.

Imprinted Impressions

In the sands of time, we etch our prose,
With laughter's echoes, and sorrows' woes,
The tides may erase, but we impose,
The marks of our passage, where life flows.

Footprints fleeting, under skies of blue,
Moments imprinted, tender and true,
Each step a story, both old and new,
In paths we've wandered, in dreams we pursue.

Carving with care, in the heart's soft clay,
Memories gather, as moonbeams play,
Silent whispers of a dawn's first ray,
Impressions linger, guiding our way.

Through storms that scatter, and winds that veer,
We script our journey, in lines sincere,
The canvas vast, neither far nor near,
Sketches of power, that persevere.

Ephemeral prints, yet timeless they stay,
In realms of the mind, and hearts that sway,
Invisible echoes, night and day,
Imprinting impressions, life's ballet.

Ephemeral Jewels

Dewdrops glisten on petals, fair,
Jewels of morning, beyond compare,
Fragile whispers in the silken air,
Moments of beauty, fleeting and rare.

Stars that shimmer, then fade to gray,
Diamonds dancing in the night's display,
Transient treasures, in a dusk-lit bay,
Glimmering secrets, till the break of day.

Mirages appear on horizon's line,
Blink and they're gone, like spilled wine,
Ephemeral jewels in a grand design,
Elusive wonders, both yours and mine.

Raindrops suspended on spider's thread,
Gems of nature, by twilight led,
Tiny prisms where colors are spread,
Fleeting splendors, by breezes fed.

Time's soft breath, through moments sweeps,
Precious seconds, in silence creeps,
Gather the jewels, the soul then keeps,
In life's short dream, where beauty sleeps.

Glimmers in the Dark

In the velvet cloak of night,
Where shadows dance in gentle light,
Glimmers whisper soft and slight,
Guiding hearts through weary plight.

Stars aflame in the cosmic sea,
Winking secrets to you and me,
Hopeful glimmers in mystery,
In their glow, we find we're free.

Candles flicker, with tender grace,
Piercing the void, in sacred space,
Each small flame, a warm embrace,
Glimmers that heal, and fears efface.

Through murky depths where dreams reside,
A spark ignites, it will not hide,
Glimmers of truth, our trusted guide,
Holding faith, as worlds collide.

In the dark, we find our spark,
Tiny lights that leave a mark,
Through the shadows, embark,
Glimmers in the dark, a lark.

Souvenirs of Silence

In the quiet of a morning's dawn,
Souvenirs of silence, gently drawn,
Unspoken words, by peace are borne,
In stillness' breath, our spirits are reborn.

Echoes soft, on a tranquil sea,
Whispered secrets, to you and me,
In the hush, our minds set free,
Finding truth in serenity.

In shadowed glen, where calm resides,
Souvenirs of silence, like gentle tides,
In the hush, where stillness guides,
Beauty in the quiet, forever abides.

Muted tones of a twilight hue,
Carry the echoes, tender and true,
Moments of silence, precious and few,
Craft souvenirs in shades of blue.

In the absence, where noise dissolves,
Peaceful insights softly revolve,
Souvenirs of silence, we resolve,
In quiet moments, our souls evolve.

Timeless Gazes

Eyes that whisper through the air,
Across the stretch of endless time,
Silent secrets they declare,
In a gaze both pure and sublime.

Moments etched in memory's stone,
Years pass yet they remain,
Softly, silently they have flown,
Yet their essence shall sustain.

Stare into eternity's face,
Find the spark of yesterday,
Love and sorrow both embrace,
In the lens of eyes that sway.

Through the windows of the soul,
Stories old and tales untold,
Depths of joy and darkened hole,
All within a gaze of gold.

Timeless as the stars above,
These gazes hold eternal grace,
Witness to life's endless love,
Eyes that time will not erase.

Intimate Stills

Whispers of lovers past and near,
Captured in a frame so tight,
Moments where no sound we hear,
Yet they glow in the softest light.

Hands that touch with tender care,
A glance that speaks of secret lore,
Silent vows forever there,
Frozen scenes forevermore.

Gentle smiles and subtle sighs,
Held within a captured square,
Silent as the evening skies,
Love's breath within the tranquil air.

Every still a story tells,
Of hearts entwined in quiet thrill,
In each shot a memory dwells,
Time stands still but moments fill.

Lovers' eyes and tender glows,
Where the heart its promise mills,
In each still, affection grows,
Bonds forever—intimate stills.

Captured Emotions

Waves of joy and seas of pain,
Held within a moment's clip,
Every tear and every gain,
Lives within a single grip.

Smiles that speak a thousand words,
Sorrows caught in silent weep,
Flying high as free as birds,
Or in depths of anguish steep.

Joyful leaps and tearful eyes,
All contained, emotions bold,
Cheeks that blush with sweet surprise,
And hands that comfort, loving hold.

Captured with a gentle click,
Reflections of the human heart,
In the lens emotions quick,
Masterpieces of life's art.

Drama in a single frame,
Every shot a burst of life,
Love and loss and fleeting fame,
Captured emotions without strife.

Instants of Gold

Fleeting moments pure as light,
Frozen in a frame of gold,
Captured in the lens's sight,
Stories of the young and old.

Summer days and winter's chill,
Springtime blooms and autumn's leaves,
Magic moments standing still,
Echoes of what heart believes.

Golden hours fast and brief,
Treasures found in seconds few,
In their sparkle, joy or grief,
Both the old and moments new.

Radiant smiles beneath the sun,
Shadows dance in moonlit glow,
Each instant, precious, every one,
In a tapestry they flow.

Glimmers of life brightly shine,
Throughout the span of years untold,
In each snapshot, love divine,
Timeless, priceless—instants of gold.

Jewels of the Past

Beneath the earth, where secrets lie,
Gems of history softly sigh.
Tales of kings and realms long gone,
Whispered through the silent dawn.

Diamonds' sparkle, ancient light,
Guides us through the endless night.
Emeralds glint like forest's peace,
From times when worries found release.

Sapphire skies of yesteryears,
Mirror laughs and forgotten tears.
Amidst these stones, stories stay,
Echoes of a bygone day.

Timeless treasures, buried deep,
In the earth's embrace they sleep.
Waiting for a hand to find,
Bringing relics to the mind.

Jewels of the past, they gleam,
In dreams of what has been, we dream.
Silent witness to life's stream,
Guardians of our ancient scheme.

Shimmering Echoes

In twilight's silent, golden glow,
Echoes of the past softly flow.
Whispers carried on the breeze,
Murmurs that our hearts appease.

Shimmering tales of love and loss,
Stretching time's unyielding gloss.
Glimpses of a bygone grace,
In every shadow, a silent trace.

Ghostly lights on waters clear,
Reflect dreams held dear.
Each glimmer tells a fabled story,
Of sorrow, hope, and fleeting glory.

The echoes dance on walls of night,
In the crescent's gentle light.
Memories swirl like drifting smoke,
Each one a tender, sacred cloak.

We listen close, to shimmering songs,
Of rights, of wrongs, of where it belongs.
Echoes fade, but still remain,
A tapestry of joy and pain.

Treasures Unveiled

Beneath the sands, in shadows deep,
Lies a treasure in endless sleep.
Locked within these ancient halls,
Stories of time, whispered calls.

Golden coins, in silence gleam,
Guardians of a distant dream.
Every jewel, a secret holds,
Histories of the valiant old.

Scrolls and maps of ages past,
Revealing truths, shadows cast.
Legends carved in timeless stone,
In a language long unknown.

Unearthed secrets spring to light,
From the dark into the bright.
Every artifact's silent claim,
Sings of glory, love, and fame.

Treasures unveiled, time's embrace,
Brings the past to present place.
A dance of epochs woven tight,
In the tapestry of night.

In the Blink of An Eye

Moments fleeting, swift as rain,
Flashing by in joy and pain.
Life's brief snapshot, quickly passed,
Eternal in each memory cast.

Stars may fall, and days may end,
Time itself a faithful friend.
In the blink of an eye, we see,
Past and future, eternally.

Every breath a silent prayer,
Each heartbeat speaks that we were there.
In a blink, the world aligns,
With whispered truths and hidden signs.

Frames of life in rapid flow,
Capture what we dearly know.
In each instant, beauty found,
Clock's sweet whisper, soft and round.

In the blink, dreams come alive,
In this fleeting, we survive.
Eternity within us lies,
In the blink of all our eyes.

Gentle Resonance

Whispers in twilight's glow,
Leaves rustle, secrets flow,
Moonlight weaves silver threads,
Nature's lullaby spreads.

Stars wink in cosmic dance,
Night's embrace, a tender trance,
Crickets sing their soft refrains,
Echoes of past summer rains.

Winds carry tales untold,
Silent promises unfold,
Beneath the ancient oak,
Memories softly evoke.

A harmony pure and sweet,
In every heart, a gentle beat,
Time's gentle hand caress,
Moments of quiet success.

Dreams drift on starlit seas,
Whispers carried by the breeze,
In this reverent silence,
Find peace, a quiet defiance.

Everlasting Shimmers

Dawn breaks in hues of gold,
Stories of old, retold,
Mountains kiss the sky,
Eagles on wings fly high.

Rivers in their endless flow,
Secrets in shadows, they bestow,
Ripples in the morning light,
Reflections pure, crystal bright.

Fields adorned in gentle green,
Life's spectrum softly seen,
Colors dance in soft embrace,
Nature's grace in every space.

Time's mystic dance unfolds,
Wisdom in whispers holds,
In every grain of sand,
Futures unknown, unplanned.

Stars in an endless array,
Guide hearts led astray,
In their radiant beams,
Lie everlasting dreams.

Ethereal Melodies

Windswept dreams take flight,
In the hush of silent night,
Notes of love softly played,
In moonlight's tender shade.

Stars hum a lullaby,
Beneath the endless sky,
Voices of the past,
In echoes, everlast.

Whispers of forgotten lore,
Oceans' rhythmic roar,
Caressing shores unknown,
In dreams, we're never alone.

Twilight's gentle kiss,
Moments of pure bliss,
Harmony in twilight gleams,
Weaver of ethereal dreams.

Every heart a song,
In night's embrace, belong,
Notes that never fade,
Eternal melodies made.

Tangible Dreams

Hopes rise with dawn's first light,
Visions clear, a wondrous sight,
Possibilities unfold,
Stories of dreams told.

Paths where shadows wane,
Journey's truths, clear and plain,
In each step, a vision gleams,
Tracing the thread of dreams.

Hands grasp what hearts believe,
In the miracles we weave,
Faith in that which seems,
To live our tangible dreams.

Mountains high, oceans wide,
Horizons where dreams abide,
Courage in every stride,
In every heart, hope is tied.

Realities crafted in light,
Where day conquers night,
In every moment, beams,
The essence of tangible dreams.

Caressing Winds

In twilight's gentle, whispering breeze,
Trees murmur softly, secrets unfreeze.
Leaves flutter lightly, a tender embrace,
Nature's symphony, our hearts trace.

Fields of gold sway, a peaceful sigh,
Mountains echo, touching the sky.
The caress of winds, a timeless dance,
Lost in the moment, a subtle trance.

Clouds drift slowly, stories they weave,
Under their shadows, the world we perceive.
The winds travel far, tales they share,
Binding the earth with love and care.

Golden Echoes

Golden rays spill, the dawn's first light,
Embroidered in morning's tender sight.
Softly whispers the world awake,
Echoes of dreams, anew to make.

Rivers glisten, a liquid gold thread,
Stories untold, by waters spread.
In the hills, where shadows play,
Golden echoes, their secrets relay.

Sunset whispers in shades of gold,
A tale of warmth, forever retold.
When night draws near, in golden hues,
Echoes linger, in twilight's muse.

Brief Whispers

Whispers float in the night's embrace,
Stars reflect on a tranquil face.
Moonlight sings through the silent air,
Brief are the whispers, but they care.

Echoes of a love forever new,
Fleeting moments felt, tender and true.
In the stillness, whispers blend,
A timeless bond, where souls mend.

Crickets sing of the secrets heard,
Under a sky where dreams are stirred.
Brief whispers fade in dawn's light,
Yet linger softly through the night.

Sunlit Shadows

In the realm where shadows play,
Sunlight dances, a bright array.
Echoes of warmth in a fleeting glance,
Where light and dark in rhythm prance.

Beneath the trees, shadows sway,
In sunlit hues, they gently lay.
A tapestry of light and shade,
Stories in silence, softly made.

Mountains stretch to touch the sky,
Casting shadows where dreams lie.
Sunlit whispers through leaves cascade,
In this world, where memories fade.

Minute Wonders

A fleeting sight of stars above,
Whispers of the moon, soft as a dove,
Every second, a story untold,
A moment's magic, in hearts to hold.

Dew upon grass at morning's first light,
Sparkles like gems, a natural delight,
Breeze kisses leaves, a gentle embrace,
Minute wonders, all over the place.

The sun dips low, painting the sky,
Colors that blend, a pleasing sigh,
Birds in chorus, herald the night,
These small marvels, simple and bright.

Raindrops dance on window panes,
Sing a tune in soft refrains,
Clouds morph in shapes, a wondrous sight,
Minute wonders, day and night.

Time moves swiftly, yet leaves behind,
Tiny treasures for hearts to find,
In the mundane, in the routine,
Minute wonders weave the unseen.

Cradled Memories

Whispers of laughter float in the air,
Remnants of joy we once did share,
In the cradle of time, they silently lie,
Memories cherished, never to die.

Old photographs, a story they tell,
Of bygone days we loved so well,
Faded colors, yet vibrant remains,
In these snapshots, life sustains.

The scent of rain on hot summer days,
Recalls those afternoons in countless ways,
Moments cradled in a tender embrace,
Memories that time cannot erase.

Echoes of voices, of songs now gone,
Lingering melodies forever drawn,
In the halls of the mind, they softly reside,
Cradled memories, forever our guide.

As shadows lengthen, as night arrive,
We find these treasures, keeping us alive,
In the cradle of love, we find our plea,
Cradled memories, forever free.

Chiseled Dreams

In the marble, visions we carve,
Dreams sculpted, we watch them starve,
Each strike of the mallet, a breath anew,
Chiseled dreams, for all to view.

In midnight's quiet, we dare to mold,
Fantastic futures, stories bold,
From raw stone, a shape emerges,
A dance of dreams, our soul purges.

With patience, with love, we define,
The edges of hope, the curves of time,
Every fragment, a small relief,
Bringing form to our belief.

We labor long, though fingers tire,
Fueled by passion, a burning fire,
In every strike, our spirit gleams,
We're artists of our chiseled dreams.

In the end, our visions stand,
Testaments to hearts and hand,
A legacy carved from silent screams,
Eternal life for our chiseled dreams.

Delicate Footprints

Tiny steps on soft, warm sand,
Traces of a journey, unplanned,
Each print, a whisper of where we've been,
Delicate footprints in a world unseen.

Across green fields, on a dew-kissed morn,
We leave our mark with feet newborn,
Silent echoes in the early light,
Footprints that dance out of sight.

In the forest, where shadows play,
We wander paths, we lose our way,
Yet behind us, a gentle trail,
Delicate footprints tell our tale.

Winter snows that softly land,
Capture our steps, a frosty strand,
In the purity of nature's glow,
Our footprints speak in silent show.

Life's journey, a fleeting song,
Yet in our steps, we linger long,
Delicate footprints, a tender tease,
The paths we tread, the memories we seize.

Ephemeral Whispers

In the quiet of dawn, whispers arise,
Carried by winds that dance with the skies.
Secrets are told in the rustling leaves,
Slipping through time like water through sieves.

Ephemeral moments that fade with the light,
Glimpses of magic in the dark of the night.
Voices of past in the murmuring streams,
Echoes of long-forgotten dreams.

The whispers that vanish as quickly as mist,
Tales that were never meant to exist.
Fleeting as shadows at the break of day,
Carried on whispers that soon drift away.

In the silence that follows a whisper's retreat,
Holds the melody of memories sweet.
A symphony played by the hands of fate,
Ephemeral whispers that don't hesitate.

Fleeting Embrace

In the twilight's gentle grace,
Love's tender, fleeting embrace.
Moments of warmth, so quickly they sway,
Just like shadows at the end of the day.

Two hearts that meet for a brief, sweet while,
Sharing a touch, a glance, a smile.
Ephemeral, yet deeply profound,
Like petals scattered upon the ground.

The embrace that lingers in memory's hold,
A story of passion quietly told.
Eyes that meet and then look away,
Promises made that cannot stay.

In the fleeting embrace, there lies a truth,
Love's essence, in its purest youth.
A whisper, a sigh, a delicate trace,
The beauty of love's fleeting embrace.

Echoes of Yesterday

In the halls where memories play,
Linger the echoes of yesterday.
Voices so faint, yet clear as a bell,
Stories they weave, tales they tell.

A laughter that dances on the breeze,
Whispers of joy in the rustling trees.
Moments suspended in time's embrace,
Reflecting the lines of every face.

Yesterday's dreams, like ripples at sea,
Gently remind us of what used to be.
Walking through shadows cast by the past,
Treasuring moments that forever last.

The echoes that follow where'er we roam,
Lingering close, they call us home.
In the silence, they softly convey,
The gentle echoes of yesterday.

Treasured Glimpses

In the journal of a heart's quiet glance,
Lie treasured glimpses of romance.
Moments of joy that, like stars, appear,
Lighting the night with memories dear.

Glimpses of laughter, of tears gently shed,
In the tapestry of a life well-led.
Seeing the past with fondness anew,
Colors that fade but never quite blue.

In the smile of a friend, a knowing look,
Treasured glimpses like pages of a book.
Fleeting, yet precious, they linger on,
Moments remembered when others are gone.

As seasons change and years slip by,
Treasured glimpses never truly die.
They remain as stars in the canvas of night,
Illuminating our hearts with their gentle light.

Veins of Time

Beneath the ancient bark, life's tale is spun,
In hidden rings, old ages past are cued.
With whispered winds, a new epoch begun,
The tree of life, in golden hues imbued.

The rivers carve through silent stone, their course,
An echo of the eons long foregone.
Through veins of time, relentless waters force,
The testament of ages carries on.

In cosmic whirl, the stars do conspire,
To write the chapters, gleaming in the dark.
Each silent witness to the endless fire,
We trace our lineage with each spark.

Eternal hands turn sands within their glass,
A measured dance, relentless as a tide.
In ceaseless march, the moments come and pass,
Each grain a story, time's unerring guide.

Adrift within the currents of the years,
We search for meaning in the temporal flow.
With eyes turned skyward, whispered hopes and fears,
We'll find our place in time's eternal glow.

Petite Mysteries

A dewdrop gleams upon the morning's crest,
A world condensed within its tiny sphere.
In solitude, a mystery manifest,
Translucent dreams in crystal form appear.

The hummingbird with iridescent flight,
Its wings a blur, a fleeting brush with grace.
In petals' folds, it drinks from morning's light,
A fragile life, a wonder to embrace.

The spider's web, an intricate design,
In threads of silk the universe is spun.
A dance of purpose in the night's decline,
The moonlight's kiss a prize for work well done.

The butterfly in quest of nectared bloom,
Its fragile wings a story yet untold.
In silent flutter, whispers through the gloom,
A metamorphosis of courage bold.

In simple things, the secrets of the earth,
Petite mysteries within our reach.
In nature's script, the tales of life and birth,
Unfolding truths that silently beseech.

Tender Resonance

A touch that lingers, soft as morning dew,
The whispered worlds within a lover's sigh.
A song of heartbeats merging two to one,
The tender resonance that defies goodbye.

A glance across the crowded room, it seems,
A spark ignites in eyes of deepest hue.
The universe compressed in silent dreams,
Within that look, a secret world anew.

The gentle caress of a sunlit breeze,
It carries warmth, a soothing, tranquil balm.
In tender moments under swaying trees,
Desires whispered in the twilight calm.

The lull of waves upon a moonlit shore,
In rhythmic dance, a soulful serenade.
With each embrace, we linger evermore,
In tender resonance where hearts are laid.

Though time may weave our paths with fates unknown,
This bond unspoken, strong as life persists.
Our shared existence, melody intone,
The tender resonance of love persists.

Sculpted Instants

Beneath the artist's hand, the marble breathes,
With every chisel, visions come to life.
In sculpted instants, time itself bequeaths,
A still perfection, free of temporal strife.

A captured smile in framed sepia tones,
The frozen laughter of a distant day.
In sculpted instants, memory intones,
A fleeting glimpse that will not fade away.

A lover's note preserved in faded script,
The ink has bled, but feelings still remain.
In sculpted instants, time's embrace is gripped,
A fleeting message carried through the strain.

A moment's pause beneath a twilight sky,
Where stars align to mark our fleeting days.
In sculpted instants, dreams begin to fly,
Eternal echoes in the cosmic maze.

Though time persists, relentless in its haste,
We carve our moments in the stone of mind.
In sculpted instants, none shall go to waste,
For in these fragments, life's true form we find.

Glimmers of Memory

In twilight's quiet, whispers low,
Fragments of yesteryears softly glow,
Threads of time, in shadows play,
Glimmers of memory, by night portray.

Old laughter in the breeze does twine,
Ghostly echoes of a bygone time,
Dreams and days, forever intertwined,
In the heart, lost pasts enshrined.

Moments flicker, here and there,
In the stillness, they ensnare,
Fading like the evening mist,
Yet in the soul, persist, persist.

Pictures painted in retreating light,
Boundless stories, whispered night,
Remnants of a once bright flame,
Particles of time's vast game.

The Tender Pause

In a moment's hush, the world does cease,
Time's swift river, frozen peace,
Breaths in sync, hearts aligned,
In the tender pause, love finds.

Eyes that meet and silently speak,
Of secrets deep and futures bleak,
Comfort in the shared still night,
Hands that hold through endless plight.

Silent whispers of the soul,
Yearnings of a heart made whole,
In this pause, they intertwine,
Hearts and hopes, a sacred sign.

Infinite the depth, within this calm,
Time is stilled by love's own balm,
In this pause, life's meaning spun,
Two hearts beat ever as one.

Captured Silence

In the quiet of a room,
Echoes of an unseen bloom,
Words unspoken, drift like mist,
In captured silence, moments kissed.

Shadows dance in candle's gleam,
Reflections of a hidden dream,
Eyes reveal the heart's delight,
In silence, love takes flight.

Muted seconds, softly slide,
In the stillness, worlds collide,
Touch the threads of whispered thought,
In silence, all is caught.

Murmurs of the silent song,
In this quiet, we belong,
Deep within the hush we share,
Captured silence, tender care.

Transient Beacons

Lights that flicker in the night,
Transient beacons, spirits bright,
Guiding ships through storm's embrace,
Seeking haven, saving grace.

From the past, they softly gleam,
Markers of a sailor's dream,
Witness to the ocean's tale,
In their glow, we set our sail.

Brief yet bold, their light does mark,
Paths through darkness cold and stark,
In their wake, the night transformed,
Hearts and hopes quietly warmed.

Though they fade with morning's rise,
Their memory lights our skies,
In the heart, forever stay,
Transient beacons, night and day.

Subdued Reflections

In the quiet moments, softly laid
Gentle whispers through the twilight fade
Moonlight dances on the rippled stream
Dreams emerge in a silver sheen.

Shadows lengthen, merging into night
Stars appear, pinpoints of distant light
Lonely echoes in the evening's breath
Memories linger, defying death.

Whispers of the past, soft and low
Navigating where the winds do blow
Flickers of a life long ago lived
In these subdued reflections, we forgive.

A journey paths through fleeting time
Tracing whispers in the day's decline
Resting here in twilight's gentle fold
Finding solace as the night grows cold.

Brief Stillness

In the hush of dawn's first light
Worlds suspended, hearts take flight
Silent whispers of a waking breeze
Sweep through branches, rustling leaves.

A pause before the day's advance
Caught within this chance of chance
Moments fleeting, breath sustained
In brief stillness, peace is gained.

Silent reflections in the mind's eye
Pondering the whys and the whys
Time surrenders to this still abode
Paths unwritten, stories untold.

Mornings dressed in quiet grace
Calm before the hurried pace
Life resumes in soft embrace
Stillness lingers, leaves its trace.

Vivid Recollections

Colors of a life intensely bright
Memories vivid in their flight
Whispers of days gone, moments held
In the heart, these recollections dwell.

Snapshot scenes in mind's refrain
Echoes of laughter, threads of pain
Portraits painted in hues so clear
Vivid recollections held so dear.

Fragments of what used to be
Merge and blend in clarity
Every detail, sharp and true
Kaleidoscope of me and you.

A canvas of moments intertwined
In every corner, treasures find
Time may fade, but memories stay
Vivid recollections light the way.

Heartfelt Raindrops

Raindrops fall, a gentle serenade
Tapping softly on the window pane
Heartfelt whispers in the stormy tide
Nature's tears and joy collide.

In each droplet, emotions poured
Thoughts and feelings, gently soared
A symphony of water and sky
Heartfelt raindrops, whispered sighs.

Drumming rhythms on the ground
Melodies in the rain abound
Drowning sorrows in the soothing sound
Heartfelt raindrops all around.

A dance of skies, a cleanse, a song
Cleansing spirits all night long
Heartfelt raindrops in the fray
Wash away the night, welcome day.

Celestial Keepsakes

Beneath the velvet sky's embrace,
The stars align in cosmic dance,
Their whispers echo, leave a trace,
Of timeless tales in night's expanse.

Eternal lights, in silence soar,
Through infinite, uncharted seas,
Their glow a message from before,
Of endless truth, and mysteries.

Galaxies waltz in silent grace,
A ballet written in the night,
Each constellation finds its place,
Amidst the dark, a beacon bright.

The moon, a guardian overhead,
Her silver beams like gentle sighs,
In dreams and slumber, we are led,
To where the cosmic secrets lie.

So gaze into the twilight deep,
And let the starlit whispers speak,
For in their glow, our spirits keep,
The secrets that our hearts bespeak.

Unseen Reverie

In shadows of the mind's domain,
Where fantasies and dreams converge,
A world unseen begins to reign,
With every whispered thought, emerge.

The silent echoes of the heart,
In this realm of figments, thrive,
Imagination plays its part,
Where unseen dreams take flight, alive.

An endless canvas, tales untold,
With vibrant strokes of color pure,
Imagined realms of old and bold,
Where nothing real can be obscure.

Lost in this reverie profound,
A sanctuary of the soul,
In endless thoughts, we're safely found,
Where fervent dreams and musings stroll.

So wander in this unseen sphere,
Let reverie and dreams collide,
For here the heart is free and clear,
In endless wonder, we'll abide.

Chronicles of Grace

Within the quiet moments spun,
An echo of a life once traced,
Each breath, a burden gently done,
In gilded chronicles of grace.

Soft whispers of a distant past,
That tell of strength in muted tones,
Each story woven strong and fast,
In time's embrace, the heart atones.

Through trials faced and battles fought,
Resilience in each tear shed,
A legacy of lessons taught,
With every step, a future led.

In kindness, courage, poise displayed,
The soul's true beauty shines so clear,
In every action, softly laid,
The chronicles of grace appear.

Let these tales be a guiding light,
Through days of joy and nights of fears,
For in the chronicles of might,
Live echoes of our yesteryears.

Subtle Embers

In the glow of fading light,
Subtle embers softly gleam,
Whispered secrets of the night,
Dance upon a twilight dream.

Flickers of a moment past,
In the hush of evening's grace,
Memories in shadows cast,
Warmth upon a gentle face.

Ebbing flames and quiet sighs,
Tell of stories now grown old,
In their glow, the past still lies,
Cloaked in amber, draped in gold.

As the night embraces still,
Embers fade but do not die,
In the heart, their warmth will fill,
Kindled by a silent sigh.

So let these embers softly burn,
In the hearth of memory,
From them, lessons we discern,
Of love and life's own reverie.

Luminous Moments

Stars whisper tales in the night,
Guiding dreams with soft light.
Moon's glow on tranquil streams,
Unveils our silent dreams.

Echoes of laughter, so bright,
In twilight, hearts take flight.
Fireflies dance, weaving spells,
In the night, magic swells.

Golden hues as dawn does break,
Nature stirs, skies awake.
Birdsong heralds day anew,
Radiant moments, pure and true.

In the daylight's tender kiss,
Find the world in gentle bliss.
Breezes murmur through the trees,
Illuminated by memories.

Twilight fades and night ascends,
A serene curtain descends.
In the dark, stillness stays,
Luminous moments gently sway.

Dreams and wonders, soft unfurled,
Awaken in a glowing world.
In the quiet of the night,
Hearts are filled with silent light.

Sacred Glows

Candles flicker in the dusk,
Incense rises, sweet and hushed.
Silent prayers, whispered low,
In sacred glows, our spirits grow.

Shadow and light dance in chapel halls,
Echoes of hymns, celestial calls.
Gentle waves of peace and grace,
In sacred glows, we find our place.

Temperate winds through stained glass,
Holy light on moments pass.
Silent awe in soft repose,
In sacred glows, the spirit knows.

An altar bathed in a golden hue,
Moments sacred, pure and true.
Time suspended, hearts align,
In sacred glows, the soul does shine.

Chants and mantras, whispered deep,
In sacred glows, secrets keep.
Ethereal light, hearts aglow,
Sacred glows, night bestows.

Journeys end in sacred light,
Blending dusk into the night.
In these glows, the spirit's flight,
Sacred warmth, forever bright.

In the Blink

In the blink, time flutters by,
Moments caught, like firefly.
Ephemeral tales, swiftly seen,
In the blink, the world serene.

Laughter lingers, like a breeze,
Frozen frames such times as these.
Happiness, a fleeting wink,
In the blink, hearts synchronize and link.

Whispers of the past remain,
In the blink, both joy and pain.
Memories dance, shadows cast,
In the blink, present becomes past.

Sunsets melt to twilight skies,
In the blink, the old goodbyes.
Seasons turn with subtle grace,
In the blink, new dawns embrace.

Precious seconds, truly fleet,
In the blink, we moments meet.
Cherish now, and hold it tight,
In the blink, day turns to night.

Through the transient we feel,
Each moment, sharp and real.
In the blink, the world unfurls,
A timeless dance, life's precious pearls.

Quiet Chronicles

Whispers of the leaves in flight,
Chronicles of day to night.
Silent tales the moon reveals,
Quiet chronicles, the heart feels.

A river's murmur, soft and low,
Chronicles of ebb and flow.
Winds weave stories through the pines,
Quiet chronicles, tender signs.

Through the meadows, shadows play,
Chronicles of light's decay.
Evening hues in silence crest,
Quiet chronicles, hearts at rest.

Starlit skies, the night unfolds,
Chronicles in silver scrolled.
Oceans whisper to the shore,
Quiet chronicles, tales of yore.

Morning dew on petals bright,
Chronicles of dawn's first light.
Nature's notes in hushed refrains,
Quiet chronicles, peace remains.

Footprints fade on sandy streams,
Chronicles of past-day dreams.
In the quiet, life's prose flows,
Quiet chronicles, softly sows.

Sacred Snapshots

In silver frames, our moments hide,
Captured whispers, time's gentle tide.
Each click a bond, forever tied,
Through lenses clear, our worlds collide.

Sunsets painted, in hues so bright,
Frozen glimpses of morning light.
In sacred snapshots, hearts take flight,
Memories dance in soft moonlight.

Children's laughter, crystal clear,
Echoes of joy, we hold so dear.
In photographs, they're always near,
In each image, love's souvenir.

Through albums worn, we trace the past,
Moments cherished, truths that last.
In sacred frames, our love's forecast,
Etched in time, steadfast, steadfast.

From novice hands to artist's eye,
We craft our stories, reach the sky.
Sacred snapshots never die,
With each glance, we breathe a sigh.

Wistful Breath

In whispered winds, she softly sighs,
An echo of the moonlit skies.
Each breath a thread that gently ties,
A wistful dream where spirit flies.

The autumn leaves, they twist and turn,
In flames of gold, they brightly burn.
With wistful breath, our hearts discern,
The silent truths we yearn to learn.

Through morning mists and twilight's gleam,
She floats upon a fragile dream.
In every sigh, a soothing stream,
Of wistful hopes, a gentle beam.

When shadows fall and stars awake,
Her breath, a tender spell does make.
In wistful realms, our pains forsake,
In whispered moments, bonds we break.

With every dawn, a chance renews,
In breath's soft cadence, we peruse.
Wistful thoughts like morning dew,
In soft reflections, find our muse.

Lasting Linger

In twilight's calm, their spirits merge,
Through silent halls, their whispers surge.
A lasting linger on the verge,
Of memories that softly urge.

Beneath the stars, their echoes swell,
In every breeze, their secrets tell.
A lasting linger casts its spell,
In moonlit nights, where shadows dwell.

They wander through the past's embrace,
In every room, they leave a trace.
A lasting linger, time's own grace,
Their presence felt, a warm solace.

In dreams they dance, a ghostly throng,
With whispered words and silent song.
A lasting linger, ever long,
In heart's deep chambers, they belong.

Through life's long path, their essence stays,
In twilight's hues and morning rays.
A lasting linger, bright displays,
Of love that binds, in endless ways.

Warmth in Passing

In fleeting moments, warmth we find,
A gentle touch, so undefined.
Through passing greets, our hearts aligned,
In fleeting warmth, our souls combined.

By fireside glows and candle's light,
We weave our stories into night.
In warmth of passing, spirits bright,
Through whispered words, we find respite.

Beneath the heavens, vast and grand,
We trace our paths, upon the sand.
In every step, we understand,
The warmth in passing, hand in hand.

As seasons change and rivers bend,
Our fleeting warmth will never end.
Through every turn, our hearts extend,
An endless warmth, a faithful friend.

In sunset's glow and morning kiss,
We find our way, in fleeting bliss.
The warmth in passing, moments miss,
Yet linger on, in timelessness.

Lifetime Fragments

Echoes of laughter, whispers of past,
Moments like glass, fragile and vast.
In memories' fabric, fragments we weave,
A tapestry of life, where dreams believe.

Time's relentless march, a steady drone,
Yet love's tender touch, a cornerstone.
Through seasons of joy and trials faced,
Lifetime fragments, beautifully traced.

From dawn's first light to twilight's end,
The journey of life, around each bend.
Moments fleeting, yet deeply ingrained,
In the heart's chamber, forever retained.

Echoes of sorrow, whispers of grace,
In life's mosaic, each piece in place.
A symphony of colors, bold and bright,
Story of a lifetime, in day and night.

In shadows of yesteryears, we find,
Footprints of the soul, intricately lined.
A map of existence, etched in time,
Fragments of a life, poetically inclined.

Opalescent Echoes

In the quiet of dawn, an opal gleams,
Whispers of secrets, woven in dreams.
Sunlight's caress, a soft embrace,
Echoes of beauty, tender and chaste.

Moonlit nights, a canvas of hues,
Stars in their dance, a celestial muse.
Each echo silent, yet profoundly deep,
A symphony of echoes, where angels weep.

Raindrops on leaves, whispers of rain,
Nature's chorus, a harmonious refrain.
Opalescent echoes, call from afar,
Melodies of stars, across the bazaar.

In the heart's enclave, silent and still,
Echoes of love, memories fill.
Each pulse a beat in the timeless expanse,
The dance of life, a trance-like dance.

In twilight's glow, where shadows play,
Opalescent echoes, night and day.
A mosaic of sounds, tender and bright,
Reflecting the heart, in purest light.

Silhouette Beneath Stars

Under the night's velvet canopy wide,
Silhouettes dance, with grace as their guide.
Stars whisper secrets, ancient and lore,
Casting their light, forevermore.

Beneath the stars, where dreams ignite,
Silhouettes weave stories in the night.
A dance of shadows, soft and mild,
In twilight's kingdom, beauty compiled.

Waves kiss the shore, gentle and slow,
Echoes of whispers, in moon's soft glow.
Silhouettes sway, in nocturnal grace,
A timeless ballet in love's embrace.

Eyes to the heavens, hearts to the ground,
In silhouettes, dreams profound.
Beneath the stars, a promise found,
In silent whispers, without a sound.

Midnight's symphony, in shadows cast,
Silhouettes await a dawn at last.
Beneath the stars, in tranquil peace,
Eternal moments, where worries cease.

Graceful Residue

In the quiet dawn, shadows retreat,
Whispers of yesterdays, bittersweet.
Life's tender touch, residue remains,
Graceful as morning, after night's rains.

Footsteps of time, gently pass,
Leaves residues, delicate as glass.
Moments of joy, sorrows too,
Graceful residue, pure and true.

Through fields of green, paths unwound,
Residues of grace, always found.
In every moment, quiet or loud,
Life's gentle imprint, makes us proud.

Breezes of time, memories sway,
Residue of life, in night and day.
Graceful echoes, softly cast,
Shadows of future, tied to the past.

Beneath the surface, deep within,
Graceful residues, where souls begin.
An endless journey, eternal quest,
In life's residue, we find our best.

Cherished Flashes

In fleeting moments, hearts do mend,
As memories in whispers blend,
A touch, a glance, a silent song,
In cherished flashes we belong.

Amid the dance of day and night,
Flashes spark in gentle light,
A laugh, a tear, the breath of spring,
In cherished flashes our souls sing.

Relics of past with future's gleam,
Meld in our hearts like woven seam,
A memory lingers, fond and warm,
In cherished flashes, love transforms.

Ephemeral Caress

The wind that whispers through the trees,
An ephemeral caress, a gentle breeze,
It holds the secrets of the past,
In traces delicate, so vast.

A fleeting sigh, a transient touch,
A moment's grace that means so much,
In shadows soft and light caress,
Ephemeral, a sweet finesse.

Beneath the stars, the night's embrace,
An evanescent, tender place,
A kiss that lingers, bittersweet,
Ephemeral caress, so fleet.

Precious Instants

In precious instants, time does freeze,
Moments captured like the breeze,
A glance, a touch, a whispered word,
In these instants, hearts are stirred.

The fleeting bloom of morning dew,
Reminds us of what we once knew,
A treasured smile, a fleeting kiss,
Precious instants, tender bliss.

Sands of time that swiftly flow,
Yet in a heartbeat, moments grow,
A memory etched, forever stayed,
In precious instants, love displayed.

Heartfelt Snapshots

Heartfelt snapshots, tender, true,
Moments captured, skies of blue,
A look, a laugh, a touch so light,
In snapshots, hearts take flight.

Through life's lens, we pause and see,
Snapshots of our history,
A day, a night, a time to share,
Heartfelt snapshots everywhere.

A silent frame, a joyous cheer,
Memories held forever near,
In the album of the mind,
Heartfelt snapshots, love defined.

Lingered Impressions

In twilight's tender, fading hue,
Memories softly reappear,
Of whispered winds and skies so blue,
Moments sweetly held dear.

Amid the rustling autumn leaves,
Ghosts of laughter, time forgot,
Each step a tale that memory weaves,
In echoes that are never lost.

Through seasons turning, swift they pass,
Yet imprints left are deep,
In every dewdrop, every glass,
Our dreams and secrets keep.

In silent thoughts of yesteryears,
We find the love that lingers,
In silent whispers, through our tears,
We trace them with our fingers.

The past and present, hand in hand,
In luminescent glow,
From forest glades to ocean sand,
Where memories softly flow.

Burnished Echoes

Underneath the starlit sky,
Glows the secret of the night,
In whispered words that never die,
In shadows cast from light.

Burnished gleam of ancient flame,
Kindled hearts and fireflies,
In every story, every name,
A spark that never dies.

Through corridors of time we tread,
Echoes of the past remain,
In laughter, love, and tears once shed,
A bright enduring chain.

Golden hues of autumn's breath,
Turned to whispers of the wind,
In the circle of life and death,
Our stories intertwine and blend.

In dreams we hear the echoes clear,
Of times that came before,
In the silence, faint yet near,
They call us evermore.

Transient Affections

In fleeting moments, hearts entwine,
With glances soft, a silent song,
A touch, a smile, a fleeting sign,
Where souls and whispers belong.

Like morning dew on petals fair,
Or sunsets fading into night,
Affections, transient as air,
Yet fill our hearts with light.

Through the days and nights we roam,
Chasing dreams and fragile peace,
In the transient, we find our home,
In love that brings release.

Moments gather, then they part,
Yet their essence always stays,
In the chambers of the heart,
Where love's soft ember lays.

In every breath and fleeting glance,
Affections come and go,
Yet in their wake, they leave a dance,
A serendipitous glow.

Infinite Silhouettes

Shadows dance in twilight's gentle hue,
Whispers of time, in patterns anew.
Contours blend, like dreams unfurled,
Infinite silhouettes, in a timeless world.

Moonlight graces the silent shore,
Echoes of yesteryear, forevermore.
Softly fading, yet ever so near,
In each shadow, a memory dear.

Stars embroider the velvet night,
Guides to the wanderers in their flight.
Figures merge, pure silhouettes,
Weaving tales we won't soon forget.

In the depths of wandering dreams,
Silhouettes whisper of hidden schemes.
Silent stories, wrapped in shade,
Infinite journeys, destinies made.

Morning sun dispels the dark,
Silhouettes fade, leaving their mark.
Yet in our hearts, they softly lie,
Infinite memories beneath the sky.

Delicate Tracings

Fingers trace the fragile glass,
Moments captured, letting time pass.
Lines so fine, like whispers shared,
Delicate tracings, of lives once bared.

Petals fall in the gentle breeze,
Softly landing, with quiet ease.
Nature's canvas, ever drawn,
Delicate tracings at the break of dawn.

Snowflakes drift in winter's chill,
Patterns fleeting, yet lingering still.
Art of nature, soft delight,
Delicate tracings in the pale moonlight.

Ripples form on a placid pond,
Echoes of where dreams have dawned.
Each curve tells of soft embrace,
Delicate tracings on water's face.

Memories etched, in light and shade,
Tracings of the paths we've made.
In the silence, they softly speak,
Delicate tracings, so tender and meek.

Muted Harmonies

Soft and low, the music sweeps,
Muted harmonies, where silence sleeps.
Notes like whispers, gently fall,
In the quiet, they tell it all.

Twilight sings to the coming night,
Muted hues in fading light.
Harmony in every sigh,
As day and night bid their goodbye.

Crickets hum in the dusky field,
Muted notes their voices yield.
Nature's choir, in soft reply,
Harmonies beneath the sky.

Heartbeats drum a whispered tune,
Underneath the pale-lit moon.
Muted songs of love and grace,
In every beat, a warm embrace.

Morning dew on silent leaves,
Holds the music the night conceives.
Muted harmonies, gentle and true,
In every dawn, there's something new.

Resonant Sparks

In the night, the stars do gleam,
Resonant sparks, like a dream.
Fires of old burn ever bright,
In every spark, a tale of light.

Flames ignite the midnight air,
Resonant sparks of a love we share.
Warmth and passion, fierce and free,
In each spark, a destiny.

Crimson sun at the break of day,
Resonant sparks in the light's first ray.
Songs of morning, bold and true,
Every spark, a world anew.

Echoes whisper through the trees,
Resonant sparks in the autumn breeze.
Each fall leaf, a spark alight,
Dancing flames in the golden light.

Candles flicker in the night's embrace,
Resonant sparks in a quiet space.
In their glow, our secrets lie,
Sparks of hope, that never die.

Evoked Warmth

In the embrace of morning light,
A gentle kiss, the sun's delight,
Casting shadows, soft and thin,
A tale of warmth, the day begins.

Every leaf, a golden hue,
Dewdrops form a radiant dew,
Whispers of a peaceful gleam,
In evoked warmth, we dream.

Flickering flames in the hearth,
Stories old, tales of mirth,
Gathered close, we share our souls,
In this warmth, our heart unrolls.

Winter's breath, it cannot chill,
The gathered warmth, where hearts fulfill,
Kindled by the love we share,
Evoked warmth is always there.

In night's cocoon, we hold it tight,
A gentle glow, through darkest night,
Memories of each warm embrace,
Evoked warmth, our saving grace.

Enlightened Minutes

In the morning hush, a silent song,
Minutes drift, yet they belong,
To those who see with open eyes,
The day's first whispers, soft arise.

Enlightened moments, pure and clear,
Each second's breath, a treasure dear,
As the clock ticks, secrets unfold,
In enlightened minutes, stories told.

Golden rays on pages cast,
Reading life's chapters, unsurpassed,
In the quiet, wisdom flows,
Enlightened minutes, softly glows.

Winds of change through time's embrace,
Minutes fleeting, leave a trace,
In each heartbeat, truths we find,
Enlightened moments, peace of mind.

As twilight fades to starry night,
Minutes glisten, soft and bright,
In the calm, reflections deep,
Enlightened minutes, gifts to keep.

Woven Threads

Tangled knots and stories spun,
In each thread, a life begun,
Fingers weave the past and now,
In this tapestry, we bow.

Colors bright and shadows deep,
Memories in fibers keep,
Every stitch, a tale unfurls,
Woven threads create our worlds.

Ancient hands and young anew,
Patterns old with something true,
In the fabric of our days,
Woven threads our spirit lays.

Through the loom, our lives entwine,
Each connection, woven fine,
In the warp and weft we find,
Woven threads of humankind.

Final piece, a vibrant spread,
Every joy and tear we've shed,
In this tapestry, all's aligned,
Woven threads, our hearts combined.

Subtle Hints

In the morning's gentle breeze,
Whispers travel through the trees,
Subtle hints of days to come,
Nature's secrets softly hum.

Through the falling autumn leaves,
Change is felt in silent eves,
Hints of winter's cool embrace,
Subtle signs in every place.

Twilight's hues in fading light,
Glimmers of the pending night,
Stars begin their quiet dance,
Subtle hints leave naught to chance.

In a word, a look, a smile,
Hints are scattered all the while,
Messages that weave and blend,
Subtle hints our hearts amend.

Every moment, whispers near,
Hints of love and fleeting fear,
In the silence, listen well,
Subtle hints have tales to tell.

Treasured Whispers

In twilight's gentle embrace, it starts,
Soft murmurs dance with lovers' hearts.
Moonbeams waltz on silken streams,
We listen close to whispered dreams.

Beneath the canopy of stars,
Secrets flutter, trace our scars.
Through shadows deep, and laughter's flare,
Each whisper, a promise, hangs in air.

The forest hums with ancient lore,
Every breeze, an echoing score.
Branches swaying, tales they tell,
In silence where these whispers dwell.

The night winds serenade our ears,
Comfort woven, soothing fears.
Treasures found in hushed refrain,
Forever held in whispered lane.

Moments treasured, hearts entwined,
Within these whispers, truth aligned.
In every breath, a story grows,
In whispered dreams, our spirit flows.

Eternal Snapshots

Moments caught in silver frames,
Life's brief flicker, transient flames.
Echoes of a fleeting glance,
Captured souls in timeless dance.

Frosted memories, vivid, bright,
Frozen time in softest light.
Laughter in the face of pain,
Snapshots frame the joy, the strain.

Candid smiles and teary eyes,
Stories held, where truth implies.
In these glimpses, heartstrings bind,
Treasures of the wandering mind.

Pages of our album spin,
Every photo, world within.
Eternal snapshots, still and pure,
Moments blend, both insecure.

As we turn, the memories fade,
Yet their essence, serenade.
Through each frame, our lives unfold,
Eternal snapshots, tales retold.

Enshrined Seconds

Glimmering moments, enshrined in time,
Each second hums a sacred rhyme.
Hands of clocks may race ahead,
Yet some seconds, never dead.

Silent reverence in heart's halls,
Every tick, a memory calls.
Enshrined seconds, vivid, bright,
Etched in soul, our guiding light.

Fleeting glimpses, sweet and brief,
Carved in stone, beyond belief.
Where whispers of the past reside,
In stillness, destiny confides.

Flashes of our sorted past,
Time's enigma, holding fast.
In enshrined seconds, truth we find,
Blessed moments, memory-lined.

Through the veil, we glimpse once more,
Seconds lost, yet we adore.
In their essence, futures gleam,
Enshrined seconds, our life's dream.

Precious Intervals

Between the heartbeats and the sighs,
Precious intervals, behind our eyes.
Measured breaths and silent breaks,
Moments sculpting all it takes.

In the pauses, life unfurls,
Spaces where the soul unfurls.
Precious intervals, soft and grand,
Filling gaps with gentle hand.

Between the laughter, between the tears,
Intervals hold cherished years.
Whispers of the softest kind,
In those gaps, our spirits find.

Time's continuum in disguise,
Moments drifting like the tides.
Intervals of love, of grace,
Beauty found in sacred space.

Within the breaths, the silent cues,
Intervals, a world imbues.
Precious gaps in life's design,
Intervals where we align.

Milton Keynes UK
Ingram Content Group UK Ltd.
UKHW050216130724
445574UK00013B/523